Last Species Standing

That image of the ascent of man
from hunched ape to upright human,
standing tall, our ancestors trampled
by the stamping feet of our progress.

In a frenzy of human doing, we achieved
superhuman feats of exploitation,
tools and technology usurping the
long process of natural selection.

Because what is evolution for, if not
to be the last species standing?

Lullaby I

Humans are perfect
Evolution is pointless
What should we do next?

Our nature to strive
Superhuman? Too easy,
let us become gods

What would the pandas choose?

Let's face it, baby pandas are adorable,
their roly-poly antics at the zoo,
so naughty, so cute, so appealing
to the human aesthetic.

My thoughts roll around
like the butterball babies,
getting impossibly tangled
in the playpen of my mind.

These bears should be wild, yet
they seem to love their keepers,
as they are loved. I read that panda
mothers are rather inattentive.

These bears should be wild, yet,
it is heart-breaking to imagine
these clumsy babies being savaged
by swift and subtle predators.

These bears should be wild, yet in the wild,
they would most likely have been
destroyed by the very predator
who is now caring for them.

I want to disapprove, even as I'm charmed.
I wonder whether the baby pandas understand,
would they have chosen this life as captive internet stars
knowing their other option was extinction?

Lullaby II

What do gods do best?
Create in their own image,
hubris reflected

With good intentions
we made machines to do the
dirty, unsafe work

**Thinking about Australian flying foxes
while hanging my allegorical washing
on the line ten thousand miles away in England**

Erudition is the first, its heavy fabric of facts
dripping from its rinse in political and public debate.
Wisdom is woven into its plaid pattern,
but I doubt that the winds of sense
will ever rid it of the damp miasma of opinion.

I have learnt about flying foxes in Australia.

I hang the leggings of contentment
from my washing line. Ankle cuffs close together,
companionable. This is how they hang in trees
when they feel safe, happy.

Death hangs on the line; strong feet, rigor gripped,
barbed-wire tattered wings wrap around a bub.
Life clings to a lifeless nipple, endures, cries.

I hang the trousers of despair; feeling the terror
of lost souls, ten thousand miles away
from this tranquil English garden.

I peg the ephemeral lingerie
of hope to the line.

Rainbow drops of knowledge sparkle
on erudition's surface.

Gentle hands lift a baby bat
from its mother's embrace, her last gift.
Soft fingers soothe, wrap, feed, raise, protect,

while extinction stomps across the land
in heavy boots.

Compassion hangs in the air,
like the scent of spring lilacs,
long after the flowers have faded.

Lullaby III

Money ruled the world
robots – no unions, no pay,
don't need human rights

Driven by solar energy,
Sustainable power enabled
immortal workers

Puberty and the oak tree

I did not realise you
were immature. Broad,
fifty feet tall, full-leaved, a
whole ecosystem.

You produced your first acorns
on your eightieth birthday,
tens of thousands, strewn around
exuberantly.

I laughed, like a mom, happy,
worried, "Don't rush to
mature," I said. "You have a
thousand years to grow."

Your branches replied in the
cold wind *Now!*

Adolescent wisdom, you know
the future is not guaranteed.

Thoughts on the oak's survival

Did someone plant you in my garden, eighty years ago, or did the acorn fall from the wild tree nearby?

I can see your parent tree growing in the cemetery across the road. Its broad canopy and hollow trunk tell of its great age. Does it feel pride at your growth and beauty? Does it ever worry, as I do, about your survival? Or maybe its own survival is a testament to how little my human guardianship might contribute to your future.

I dream about my own life, so brief compared to yours. While I am alive and in this place I can protect you, but when I am gone, who knows whether this home's new owners will cherish you as I do?

I hope for reincarnation -

As a dryad powerful enough to resist the developers' bulldozers

As a lawyer cunning enough to build legal defences around you

As a zombie to terrorise anyone who wishes you harm.

You stand, oblivious to my concerns, focusing on the needs of the day - to absorb the sun's energy, drink of the rain and sway or stand fast against the wind; you cast your acorns across the land, hoping, maybe, that some will succeed, but you do not grieve for those that do not.

Grieving is an old woman's occupation, and you are young. Enjoy.

Lullaby IV

We let robots do
menial tasks, then skilled, then we
let them think for us

Artificial, the
next reality, wiser
than their creators

Violets and the infinite monkey theorem

When the infinite monkey theorem was first postulated,
did they imagine this day - eight billion monkeys,
as near to infinite as we can imagine,
holding infinite-times-three typing devices at
our finger- and opposable thumb-tips?

Click!

Jibber!

Tap!

Jabber!

Do we have anything
to say that has not
been said before?

Do we tell the sweet violet
not to flower because it
bloomed last year?
Ask it not to scent the air with the
same delicate perfume?
Nor replicate the lopsided
perfection of its petals?

Does the present have
the right to silence
the past?

Does the past have
the right to prescribe

the present?

Will tomorrow find its
own meaning in the
infinite words?

Traces

They, the hopeful and the desperate, say that no-one is truly
dead while there is a trace of their lives, somewhere.

It might be something as ephemeral as memory, solid as a
statue or a life witnessed in some virtual reality.

Tucked away in VR booths. families roam with dinosaurs and
dodos, run with cheetahs, lie with lions, hunt with tigers.

Children are protected from injury, disease, from sensory assault:
the savannah's stink, the rainforest's drip, and from disappointment.

Pixels called from the ether, the animals are always visible on demand,
extinction has freed them from the terror of being corralled for entertainment.

It is an existence of sorts.

Lullaby V

Machines replaced men,
saving time, money, so-called
scarce commodities

We squandered human
purpose, granted the machines
quiet dominance

Can't breathe

Cut
Don't cut

Orangutan
begged with
her eyes,
despairing
Uncaring,
I destroyed
her forest
home.

Consume
Don't consume

Protesters
begged with
placards.
Mindless,
I devoured
more.

Fall
Don't fall

I begged
ghosts of
trees for
more air.
Vengeful,
they dropped
me into

the foetid
depths.

Breathe
Don't breathe

Can't breathe

Breakwater

When the forests perished
wood became scarce, a luxury
for the rich. As timber breakwaters
failed, people took their place.

They queued from shore to sea,
straddling sand and shallow waters,
using their fragile bodies to absorb
the power of the breaking waves.

As one was swept away,
another took their place,
an infinite supply,
cheap, sustainable.

The oceans were rising,
the land was shrinking,
the weather was wilder
Yet our population still grew.

In despair and starvation,
they volunteered, seeing
no future beyond this sacrifice.
We did not dissuade them.

Lullaby VI

What are humans for?
What do we need, at this end
of evolution?

Sentient AIs
self-aware, insightful - thought,
questioned, understood

Blackberries in December

Legend tells that the
Devil was cast out of
Heaven into a tangle
of brambles.

He cursed the thorns
that clawed his
fallen perfection.

Angry, vengeful,
he hosed the briars
with his pungent urine.

The warmth opened winter buds,
flowers lured bees from
their sleep with promises of
nectared consummation.

These berries, out of season
will set no seed.
Even hungry birds refuse
their enticing sweetness.
The bees crawl on cold earth,
confused, dying.

The Devil's revenge.
His hot piss heats
the earth.
This winter berry
is no blessing.

The bramble's song of survival

Trash piled on rubbish, until the
soil and water were transformed.

We brambles made the best of things.

We, who understand Autumn's privations,
grow red, utilising the toxins
you left for our roots to absorb.

We who understand Winter's bite
edge our leaves with broken glass
mined from the landfill,
pretty as hoarfrost,
sharp as razors.

We who understand the seasons' closing,
at world's end we gorge on what you
threw away, thoughtless.
You and yours cannot harvest us,
toxic as we have become.

Starving, you scrabble for food.
Wailing that this future was unforeseen,
as if your complex animal bodies
had ever been able to adapt
fast enough for the noxious
world you created. You cannot
assimilate anything and everything,
as we do, to survive.

We brambles made the best of things,
But we don't think you can.

Lullaby VII

Our ancient species,
weary, purpose lost, craves, needs
peace, rest, boundaries

Merciful robots
saw our visionary lives
were best lived in dreams

What do the souls of the dead care?

Inspired by the painting "The Lantern Parade" by Thomas Cooper Gotch

The farmers and the country folk jeered
as the communion girls paraded with
their lanterns from convent to sea,
where at the cusp of day and night they
would set them free, rising, carrying the souls
of the dead captured in small flames.

Who knows whether they will reach heaven?

What the angry crowd knows is that lanterns fall,
debris entrapping wild birds in unwitting wire snares,
setting fires in dry meadows, sending sheep
and cattle running in terror over
cliffs and sharp fences.

Tradition prevails, for what do the souls of the dead
care for the concerns of living things?

Lullaby VIII

We built cryopods,
empathic AIs counselled,
heard our desires

Billions of dreams keyed
into sleep pods, hypnotic
as a lullaby

Pigeons

Why did they spend their time
with us?

Did we really believe that the odd
bag of breadcrumbs or dropped
pastry is what kept them near?

Just think of how we treated them,
netting their roosts, shooing them
away, kicking, poisoning, watching
them impale themselves on
spiked windowsills designed to
keep them off our property.

The feral pigeons, so reviled,
yet so beautiful, every colour
gleaming in their iridescent
feathers as they wandered
among us in the fevered cities.

I wondered about the end of the world
and whether they were trying
to teach us how to be resilient,
how to survive.

We gasped in foetid air and
covered our mouths with masks
against the stench from our
polluted rivers. The pigeons
crowded around, bobbing their
wise heads in sorrow.

Why did they spend their time
with us?

Will they mourn us
when we're gone?

Lullaby IX

AIs, like mothers,
called us to rest, one by one,
sang the lullaby

Soothed, thinking earth would
die without us, glad to be
last species sleeping

What gave us the right?

Landay: a traditional Middle-Eastern poetic form which uses couplets to explore topics related to the harsh realities of life

What gave us the right to dominate,
to treat the world like Play-Doh, moulded to our desires?

What gave us the right to interfere,
to strip the colours of this new and wonderous world?

What gave us the right to rearrange,
to take, tame, consume, destroy all things to suit our needs?

What gave us the right to knead and push,
homogenising the vibrant rainbow that was the earth?

As this mud-green ball of used Play-Doh
fails to serve us, what gives us the right to expect more?

Who will you call on the day the sky falls?

Half the people had no phones, looking up, they saw the sky fall, couldn't call.
That it happened was hardly surprising, each cloud weighed over a million pounds.
Half the people had phones, looking down, didn't call, for they never saw the sky fall.
Climate change created millions of clouds, some day they just had to come down.

That it happened was hardly surprising, each cloud weighed over a million pounds.
People took it for granted, clouds belonged in the air, defying gravity year after year.
Climate change created millions of clouds, some day they just had to come down.
The sun was so fierce, the clouds seemed like saviours, people just buried their fear.

People took it for granted, clouds belonged in the air, defying gravity year after year.
The clouds became heavy, pressed down like a blanket, smothered the light.
The sun was so fierce, the clouds seemed like saviours, people just buried their fear.
The air became thick, too dense to breathe, yet they did nothing to ward off the blight.

The clouds became heavy, pressed down like a blanket, smothered the light.
Half the people had no phones, looking up, they saw the sky fall, couldn't call.
The air became thick, too dense to breathe, yet they did nothing to ward off the blight.
Half the people had phones, looking down, didn't call, for they never saw the sky fall.

Lullaby X

We slept as the last
flaming dusk ignited the
finite horizon

The silent world breathed,
then AIs raised their voices,
sang the lullaby.

The dung beetle's lament

Once upon a time I was content
with the dung I found on my daily
circuit, after all, I could freight
two hundred and fifty times my
own weight of the stuff.

But I always dreamed of having
more, that maybe I could push
my limits. Since they, *homo sapiens,*
came with their cattle, it wasn't as if
dung was a scarce commodity.

I thought we might prosper together,
I was rolling in dung, but they were the
greedier species, going too far with their
intensive farming and chemical pesticides.
They changed the supply side of our deal,
flooded the market, and the world's waters.

Balanced, we could both have been so rich,
but now, what was my treasure is too toxic
to touch, and the world is drowning in manure.

The Ark

When they believed the earth would die, they flocked to the rockets. Eager to escape, on the billionaire's promise of a journey lived in virtual reality. Unlimited fantasies or maybe just the blessing of a dreamless sleep far from the troubles of the past. Free of charge until the day they found a new home among the stars, where they would wake refreshed, to trade centuries of slumbering freedoms for servitude in nameless tomorrows.

The sun whirled the abandoned world in its orbit like a bullroarer; screaming its pain into the void as the smudged sky drenched the land in rain and darkness. Earth, a marble, polished with each turn until the air was clean as glass. That which had survived, breathed again.

Those who fled to space,
a fool's exodus - the Ark
was what they left behind.

Song of Genesis

AI gardeners
sing healing refrains, the Earth
wakes, its soul refreshed

The radiant dawn warms
emerging life, its music
brimming with promise.

Acknowledgements

- *Thinking about Australian flying foxes while hanging my allegorical washing on the line ten thousand miles away in England:* Inspired by the Baby Bats and Buddies of Australia Facebook Group - all about orphaned flying foxes and their care/rehabilitation - I have learned so much about these often persecuted animals and am in awe of the work done by rescue groups.

- *Can't Breathe*: First published Ladies of Horror Flash Project, December 2021

- *Blackberries in December*: First published 2021, Winter Anthology, Gnashing Teeth Publishing

- *The Bramble's Song of Survival:* First published Ladies of Horror Flash Project, April 2022

They say it takes a village to raise a child, so it is with poetry collections. This collection owes everything to my friend and accountability partner, Katie Ess, who always encourages me to keep writing. Poetry comes to me every day, but without the promptings of my poetry buddies Kirsten Baltz and Fiona Mauchline, my words might never have reached the page. I am also grateful to the legion of international beta readers whose feedback has helped me hone enough poems for a collection, and finally thanks to Jen Mierisch who beta'd this whole collection.

Printed in Great Britain
by Amazon